Editor
Eric Migliaccio

Editor in Chief
Ina Massler Levin, M.A.

Creative Director
Karen J. Goldfluss, M.S. Ed.

Illustrator
Renée Mc Elwee

Cover Artist
Brenda DiAntonis

Art Coordinator
Renée Mc Elwee

Imaging
Rosa C. See
Craig Gunnell

Publisher
Mary D. Smith, M.S. Ed.

Grade 3

ANALOGIES
for
Critical Thinking

TCR 3166

insect : ladybug

mammal : cat

A terrific way to:

* Sharpen logical thinking skills
* Prepare for standardized tests
* Understand word relationships
* Improve & develop vocabulary

Teacher Created Resources

Author

Ruth Foster, M.Ed.

Teacher Created Resources
12621 Western Avenue
Garden Grove, CA 92841
www.teachercreated.com
ISBN: 978-1-4206-3166-1
©2011 Teacher Created Resources
Reprinted, 2016
Made in U.S.A.

Teacher Created Resources

Table of Contents

Introduction

Think of an analogy as a wonderful puzzle, and one has a great interdisciplinary teaching exercise.

An analogy is a type of comparison. An analogy is when a likeness is found between two unlike things. If approached as a puzzle, one solves the analogy by finding out how the pieces fit together. What links the words to each other? How can they be connected or tied together? What is the relationship between them?

cat is to **meow** as **dog** is to ___**bark**___

Although the example above may appear to be easy, it is an exercise that involves cognitive processes and critical-thinking skills. One must comprehend the words read, categorize them, understand the connection between them, and then find a similar connection between a different pair of words. In this case, both *meow* and *bark* are sounds that a cat and dog make, respectively.

Analogies written for this series will focus on a variety of word relationships. They will develop, reinforce, and expand skills in the following areas:

→ visual imagery

→ reading comprehension

→ paying attention to detail (word sequence within word pairs)

→ vocabulary development

→ synonym, antonym, and homophone recognition and recall

→ understanding different shades of word meanings

→ reasoning

→ standardized-test taking

Students will be able to demonstrate mastery by doing the following:

→ working with both multiple-choice and write-out question formats

→ analyzing and fixing incorrect analogies

→ writing their own analogies in both question and sentence format

For interdisciplinary practice, some analogies will be subject-specific (addressing science, math, or social studies, for example). Others will push students to think outside of the box, as creative and imaginative connections between words will be asked for. Students may then explain in writing or verbally (depending on skill level) how they created analogous word pairs or situations.

Blank answer sheets can be found on page 60. Use these sheets to provide your students with practice in answering questions in a standardized-test format.

Introducing Analogies

Directions: Fill in the word you think should go in the blank.

1. **Cat** is to **kitten** as **dog** is to ___Puppy___.
2. **Cat** is to **meow** as **dog** is to ___Bark___.
3. **Cat** is to **paw** as **person** is to ___hand___.
4. **Cat** is to **fur** as **bird** is to ___feathers___.
5. **Cat** is to **tame** as **lion** is to ___wild___.

What did you just do? You made analogies! An **analogy** is a likeness in some way between things that are otherwise unlike.

A kitten is not a puppy. A kitten is like a puppy, however, because they are both babies.

Sometimes analogies are written like this:

> **cat : kitten :: dog : puppy**

- The single colon (**:**) compares two items in a word pair.
- The double colon (**::**) compares the first word pair to the second word pair.

---

6. Rewrite question 2, 3, 4, *or* 5 in the analogy form.

   ___Cat___ : ___Kitten___ :: ___Dog___ : ___puppy___

Directions: Fill in the blanks to finish the analogies.

7. boy : girl :: mother : ___father___
8. boy : girl :: dad : ___mom___
9. boy : girl :: uncle : ___Aunt___
10. boy : girl :: man : ___woman___

Synonyms in Analogies

A **synonym** is a word that is nearly the same in meaning as another word.

1. Which word is not a synonym of the others?

   Ⓐ small   Ⓑ tiny   Ⓒ big *(circled)*   Ⓓ little

2. Which answer makes the best analogy?

   Ⓐ small : tiny :: big : little   Ⓒ big : small :: teeny : little

   Ⓑ small : little :: teeny : tiny *(circled)*   Ⓓ teeny : big :: little : small

---

Directions: Fill in the circle next to the synonym that best completes the analogy.

3. **Speedy** is to **fast** as **pretty** is to ___beautiful___ .

   Ⓐ nice   Ⓑ quick   Ⓒ silly   ● beautiful

4. **Trap** is to **catch** as **yell** is to ___shout___ .

   Ⓐ shut   Ⓑ should   ● shout *(circled)*   Ⓓ shell

5. **Come** is to **enter** as **leave** is to ___exit___ .

   ● exit   Ⓑ stay   Ⓒ race   Ⓓ place

6. **Smelly** is to **stinky** as **rest** is to ___Relax___ .

   Ⓐ smart   Ⓑ part   Ⓒ piece   ● relax

7. **Funny** is to **silly** as **chatty** is to ___talkative___ .

   ● talkative   Ⓑ chilly   Ⓒ silent   Ⓓ breezy

8. **Dull** is to **boring** as **exciting** is to ___thrilling___ .

   Ⓐ tiring   Ⓑ simple   Ⓒ foolish   ● thrilling

Directions: Create four answers for this analogy. Only one answer should be correct!

9. **Big** is to **enormous** as **cruel** is to ___mean___ .

   Ⓐ ___Punnishing___   Ⓒ ___angry___

   Ⓑ ___Rude___   Ⓓ ___mean___

10. Which one of your answers was correct? Write a sentence telling why. Use the word *synonym* in your sentence.

   ___Mean was the correct answer because mean___
   ___is the synonym of cruel___

©Teacher Created Resources   5   #3166 Analogies for Critical Thinking

Antonyms in Analogies

An **antonym** is a word that is the **opposite** in meaning of another word.

1. Which word is an antonym of the others?

   Ⓐ baked   Ⓑ cooked   Ⓒ roasted   Ⓓ **raw**

2. Which answer makes the best analogy?

   Ⓐ **cooked : raw :: fast : slow**   Ⓒ roasted : raw :: strange : odd

   Ⓑ raw : baked :: tired : sleepy   Ⓓ raw : cooked :: silly : funny

---

Directions: Find the antonym that best completes the analogy.

3. **Hot** is to **cold** as **dirty** is to _____.

   Ⓐ messy   Ⓑ clean   Ⓒ **filthy**   Ⓓ chilly

4. **Old** is to **young** as **cowardly** is to _____.

   Ⓐ shy   Ⓑ timid   Ⓒ ancient   Ⓓ **brave**

5. **Dull** is to **exciting** as **tasty** is to _____.

   Ⓐ thrilling   Ⓑ tiring   Ⓒ **bland**   Ⓓ hot

6. **Hard** is to **soft** as **simple** is to _____.

   Ⓐ easy   Ⓑ **difficult**   Ⓒ funny   Ⓓ foolish

7. **Awake** is to **asleep** as **stay** is to _____.

   Ⓐ play   Ⓑ exercise   Ⓒ **depart**   Ⓓ nap

8. **Most** is to **least** as **yell** is to _____.

   Ⓐ **whisper**   Ⓑ shout   Ⓒ scream   Ⓓ sing

Directions: Create four answers for this analogy. Only one answer should be correct!

9. **Sad** is to **happy** as **cheerful** is to _boring_.

   Ⓐ _glum_   Ⓒ _lazy_

   Ⓑ _boring_   Ⓓ _tiring_

10. Which one of your answers was correct? Write a sentence telling why. Use the word *antonym* in your sentence.

    Boring is correct bec aus boring is the antonym of cheerful

Synonym and Antonym Practice

Directions: First, fill in the circle of the answer that best completes the analogy. Then, write **S** for *synonym* or **A** for *antonym* on the blank line to describe how the question and answer words are related. The first one has been done for you. Remember . . .

- Antonyms are words that are opposite in meaning.
- Synonyms are words that mean the same.

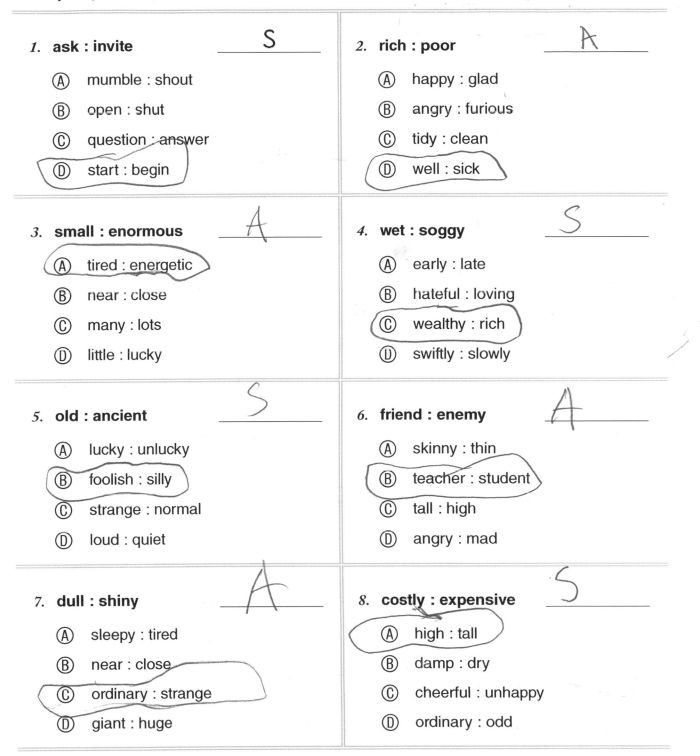

1. **ask : invite** _____S_____
   - (A) mumble : shout
   - (B) open : shut
   - (C) question : answer
   - (D) start : begin

2. **rich : poor** _____A_____
   - (A) happy : glad
   - (B) angry : furious
   - (C) tidy : clean
   - (D) well : sick

3. **small : enormous** _____A_____
   - (A) tired : energetic
   - (B) near : close
   - (C) many : lots
   - (D) little : lucky

4. **wet : soggy** _____S_____
   - (A) early : late
   - (B) hateful : loving
   - (C) wealthy : rich
   - (D) swiftly : slowly

5. **old : ancient** _____S_____
   - (A) lucky : unlucky
   - (B) foolish : silly
   - (C) strange : normal
   - (D) loud : quiet

6. **friend : enemy** _____A_____
   - (A) skinny : thin
   - (B) teacher : student
   - (C) tall : high
   - (D) angry : mad

7. **dull : shiny** _____A_____
   - (A) sleepy : tired
   - (B) near : close
   - (C) ordinary : strange
   - (D) giant : huge

8. **costly : expensive** _____S_____
   - (A) high : tall
   - (B) damp : dry
   - (C) cheerful : unhappy
   - (D) ordinary : odd

Synonym and Antonym Analogies

Directions: Write as many synonyms and antonyms as you can think of for the given words. If you want, you may use a thesaurus.

	Synonyms	Antonyms
1. big	large giant huge	small tiny teenie
2. rich	wealthy well-of	Poor needy wanting
3. brave	bravely no-fear	chicken coward cowardly
4. silly	birdbrained gooty	serious-minded
5. sad	gloomy glum joyless	cheerful cheery happy

Directions: Write two analogy questions using some of the words you wrote down. One question should be a synonym. The other question should be an antonym.

6. _____ : _____

  Ⓐ _____ : _____

  Ⓑ _____ : _____

  Ⓒ _____ : _____

  Ⓓ _____ : _____

Synonym or antonym? _____

Correct answer _____

7. _____ : _____

  Ⓐ _____ : _____

  Ⓑ _____ : _____

  Ⓒ _____ : _____

  Ⓓ _____ : _____

Synonym or antonym? _____

Correct answer _____

Plurals

Plural means "more than one." When making some words plural . . .

- add *es* to some words ending in *o*. (**Example:** potato — potatoes)
- change *f* to *v* and add *s* or *es* to words ending in an *f* or *fe*. (**Example:** wife — wives)

Directions: Write in the correct answer to complete the analogies.

1. **Potato** is to **potatoes** as **tomato** is to ___tomatoes___ .

2. **Wife** is to **wives** as **half** is to ___halves___ .

3. **Leaf** is to **leaves** as **wolf** is to ___wolves___ .

4. **Life** is to **lives** as **knife** is to ___knives___ .

5. **Self** is to **selves** as **loaf** is to ___loaves___ .

6. **Veto** is to **vetoes** as **volcano** is to ___volcanoes___ .

7. **Burglar** is to **burglars** as **thief** is to ___thieves___ .

8. **Calf** is to **calves** as **elf** is to ___elves___ .

9. **Shelf** is to **shelves** as **hoof** is to ___hooves___ .

10. **Echo** is to **echoes** as **hero** is to ___heroes___ .

11. Which question uses synonyms? ___Burglar is to burglars as thief is to___

Challenge: Try to make up a sentence that uses four or more of the bolded words used in the questions. The words can be singular or plural.

_____

_____

Plurals 2

1. Use the same words, but rewrite this analogy so it is correct.

children : child :: man : men

Children : child :: men : man

Directions: Choose the answer that best completes each analogy. Pay attention to the order and spelling of single and plural words!

2. **knife : knives**

- (A) ox : oxes
- (B) ox : oxen
- (C) oxes : ox
- (D) oxen : ox

3. **volcanoes : volcano**

- (A) childs : child
- (B) child : childs
- (C) tooth : teeth
- (D) teeth : tooth

4. **wolf : wolves**

- (A) goose : geese
- (B) geese : goose
- (C) leaf : leafs
- (D) leafs : leaf

5. **echo : echoes**

- (A) tomato : tomatos
- (B) tomatos : tomato
- (C) person : people
- (D) people : person

6. **thieves : thief**

- (A) wifes : wife
- (B) wife : wifes
- (C) mice : mouse
- (D) mouse : mice

7. **heroes : hero**

- (A) feet : foot
- (B) foot : feet
- (C) potatos : potato
- (D) potato : potatoes

8. **man : men**

- (A) echos : echo
- (B) echo : echos
- (C) women : woman
- (D) woman : women

9. **lives : life**

- (A) mouse : mice
- (B) mice : mouse
- (C) house : hice
- (D) hice : house

10. What is the correct way to spell the plural of *house*? _____

A Trip to the Zoo

Directions: Think about the sounds animals make at the zoo. Then choose the answer that best completes each analogy. Pay attention to order!

1. **sheep : baa**
   - (A) animal : sound *(circled)*
   - (B) sound : animal

2. **baa : sheep**
   - (A) animal : sound
   - (B) sound : animal *(circled)*

3. **sheep : baa**
   - (A) neigh : cow
   - (B) cow : neigh
   - (C) neigh : horse
   - (D) horse : neigh *(circled)*

4. **donkey : bray**
   - (A) goose : honk *(circled)*
   - (B) honk : goose
   - (C) duck : bark
   - (D) bark : duck

5. **trumpet : elephant**
   - (A) hyena : laugh
   - (B) laugh : hyena *(circled)*
   - (C) zebra : roar
   - (D) roar : zebra

6. **owl : hoot**
   - (A) frog : moan
   - (B) moan : frog
   - (C) crow : caw *(circled)*
   - (D) caw : crow

7. **duck : quack**
   - (A) dove : coo *(circled)*
   - (B) quack : duck
   - (C) moo : cow
   - (D) bleat : goat

8. **peep : chick**
   - (A) bray : puppy
   - (B) dog : bark
   - (C) meow : kitten *(circled)*
   - (D) cat : meow

9. **roar : tiger**
   - (A) parrot : screech
   - (B) cricket : chirp
   - (C) quack : monkey
   - (D) grunt : warthog *(circled)*

10. **snake : hiss**
    - (A) boar : croak
    - (B) ram : neigh
    - (C) stallion : moo
    - (D) rooster : crow *(circled)*

11. **Think and Write:** What is the loudest, strangest, or scariest animal sound you have ever heard? Tell when and where you heard it.

Animals on the Loose

Directions: Think about how animals move. Then, choose the answer that best completes each analogy. Pay attention to order!

1. **slither : snake**
   - Ⓐ animal : how moves
   - Ⓑ how moves : animal

2. **snake : slither**
   - Ⓐ animal : how moves
   - Ⓑ how moves : animal

3. **fish : swims**
   - Ⓐ jellyfish : floats
   - Ⓑ floats : jellyfish
   - Ⓒ starfish : floats
   - Ⓓ floats : starfish

4. **horse : gallops**
   - Ⓐ tortoise : hops
   - Ⓑ hops : tortoise
   - Ⓒ rabbit : hops
   - Ⓓ hops : rabbit

5. **monkey : swings**
   - Ⓐ marches : ant
   - Ⓑ ant : marches
   - Ⓒ lizard : dives
   - Ⓓ dives : lizard

6. **butterfly : flits**
   - Ⓐ cow : trots
   - Ⓑ trots : cow
   - Ⓒ soars : hawk
   - Ⓓ hawk : soars

7. **jumps : kangaroo**
   - Ⓐ cheetah : races
   - Ⓑ crawls : beetle
   - Ⓒ deer : bounds
   - Ⓓ squirms : fly

8. **waddles : duck**
   - Ⓐ whale : breaches
   - Ⓑ goose : jumps
   - Ⓒ wiggles : camel
   - Ⓓ dives : pelican

9. **bluebird : fly**
   - Ⓐ emu : soar
   - Ⓑ ostrich : run
   - Ⓒ walk : kiwi
   - Ⓓ swim : penguin

10. **dolphin : leaps**
    - Ⓐ elephant : floats
    - Ⓑ camel : bounds
    - Ⓒ reindeer : prances
    - Ⓓ jumps : frog

11. **Think and Write:** A penguin cannot fly. Yet people say that penguins can fly through the water. Why do you think this is so?

_____

_____

Past and Present

A **verb** is an **action** word. A verb tells you what you are doing. Verbs have different tenses.

- The **present tense** is used for an action that is happening now.
- The **past tense** is used for an action that has already happened.

Directions: Look at the examples of verbs. Write down two more examples.

Present	Past
ride	rode
write	wrote
run	ran
dig	dug

Directions: Choose a word from the word box that best completes each analogy.

rose	speed	hurt
see	bled	walk
taught	gazed	
searched	find	

1. become : became :: teach : taught

2. look : looked :: gaze : gazed

3. knew : know :: saw : see

4. dance : danced :: bleed : bled

5. thought : think :: found : find

6. give : gave :: search : searched

7. cut : cut :: hurt : hurt

8. led : lead :: walked : walk

9. send : sent :: rise : rose

10. spoke : speak :: sped : speed

11. Write down the question numbers of the ones that were . . .

- present to past 1. 2. 4. 9.
- impossible to tell 7
- past to present 3. 5. 6. 8. 10
- synonyms _____

Past and Present 2

Some analogies are based on past and present verb tenses. Something **past** has already happened. Something **present** is happening now.

Directions: Choose the answer that best completes each analogy. Pay attention to order!

1. **buy : bought**
   - (A) present : past
   - (B) past : present

2. **bought : buy**
   - (A) present : past
   - (B) past : present

3. **eat : ate :: choose :**
   - (A) choses
   - (B) chose
   - (C) chosing
   - (D) chosed

4. **sit : sat :: creep :**
   - (A) creeps
   - (B) creeping
   - (C) crept
   - (D) creeper

5. **came : come**
   - (A) dug : dig
   - (B) dig : dug
   - (C) felt : feeling
   - (D) feeling : felt

6. **heard : hear**
   - (A) listen : listens
   - (B) listens : listen
   - (C) kept : keep
   - (D) keep : kept

7. **leave : left**
   - (A) trying : tries
   - (B) tries : trying
   - (C) wept : weep
   - (D) weep: wept

8. **fell : fall**
   - (A) tore : tear
   - (B) tear : tore
   - (C) rip : rips
   - (D) rips : rip

9. Write down the past and present tense of two verbs. The verbs you list should not be in the questions above.

	Present	Past
1.		
2.		

10. Make an analogy using your verbs from Question 9.

   _____ : _____ :: _____ : _____

Purpose

Some analogies are based on how things can be used, or what their purposes are.

Directions: Choose the answer that best completes each analogy. Pay attention to order!

---

1. scissors : cut

- (A) thing : use
- (B) use : thing

2. cut : scissors

- (A) thing : use
- (B) use : thing

---

3. spoon : stir :: book :

- (A) sip
- (B) throw
- (C) read
- (D) plate

4. smell : nose :: hear :

- (A) mouth
- (B) face
- (C) foot
- (D) ear

---

5. brush : paint

- (A) write : pencil
- (B) pencil : write
- (C) finger : hand
- (D) hand : finger

6. phone : call

- (A) cut : paper
- (B) paper : cut
- (C) jump : rope
- (D) rope : jump

---

7. bake : oven

- (A) float : raft
- (B) raft : float
- (C) bike : car
- (D) car : bike

8. draw : crayon

- (A) red : orange
- (B) orange : red
- (C) sip : straw
- (D) straw : sip

---

9. List two things. Write down their purpose. The things you list should not be in the questions above.

	Thing	Purpose
1.		
2.		

10. Make an analogy using your answers from Question 9.

_____ : _____ :: _____ : _____

Where Things Go

Some analogies are based on where things go, where they live, or where they are found.

Directions: Choose the answer that best completes each analogy. Pay attention to order!

1. **wall : picture**
   - Ⓐ thing : where goes
   - Ⓑ where goes : thing

2. **picture : wall**
   - Ⓐ thing : where goes
   - Ⓑ where goes : thing

3. **dress : closet :: rug :**
   - Ⓐ roof
   - Ⓑ carpet
   - Ⓒ window
   - Ⓓ floor

4. **car : road :: train :**
   - Ⓐ track
   - Ⓑ engine
   - Ⓒ land
   - Ⓓ crossing

5. **bed : boy**
   - Ⓐ fire : red
   - Ⓑ red : fire
   - Ⓒ crib : baby
   - Ⓓ baby : crib

6. **kitchen : stove**
   - Ⓐ library : book
   - Ⓑ book : library
   - Ⓒ oven : refrigerator
   - Ⓓ refrigerator : oven

7. **boat : water**
   - Ⓐ air : plane
   - Ⓑ plane : air
   - Ⓒ bird : seeds
   - Ⓓ seeds : bird

8. **water : glass**
   - Ⓐ milk : white
   - Ⓑ white : milk
   - Ⓒ vase : flower
   - Ⓓ flower : vase

9. List two things. Write down where they go, live, or are found. The things you list should not be in the questions.

	Thing	Where Thing Goes, Lives, or Is Found
1.		
2.		

10. Make an analogy using your answers from Question 9.

_____ : _____ :: _____ : _____

Family Names

Some analogies are based on the names of old, young, male, and female family members.

Directions: Choose the answer that best completes each analogy. Pay attention to order!

1. **dog : puppy**

  Ⓐ old : young

  Ⓑ young : old

2. **puppy : dog**

  Ⓐ old : young

  Ⓑ young : old

3. **cat : kitten :: horse :**

  Ⓐ foal

  Ⓑ baby

  Ⓒ stallion

  Ⓓ mare

4. **mom : dad :: aunt :**

  Ⓐ mother

  Ⓑ uncle

  Ⓒ brother

  Ⓓ grandmother

5. **duck : duckling**

  Ⓐ sister : brother

  Ⓑ brother : sister

  Ⓒ gosling : goose

  Ⓓ goose : gosling

6. **calf : fawn**

  Ⓐ deer : cow

  Ⓑ cow : deer

  Ⓒ sheep : horse

  Ⓓ horse : sheep

7. **rooster : hen**

  Ⓐ piglet : lamb

  Ⓑ lamb: piglet

  Ⓒ buck : doe

  Ⓓ doe : buck

8. **ewe : lamb**

  Ⓐ mare : foal

  Ⓑ foal : mare

  Ⓒ sheep : ram

  Ⓓ ram : sheep

9. A *colt* is a boy baby horse. A *filly* is a girl baby horse. Make up an analogy where you use the words *colt* and *filly*. Make sure only one answer is correct. You may use words from the other questions if you want.

_____ **:** _____

  Ⓐ _____ **:** _____   Ⓒ _____ **:** _____

  Ⓑ _____ **:** _____   Ⓓ _____ **:** _____

10. What answer was correct? Tell why. _____

_____

Adjectives

Adjectives are often used in analogies. An **adjective** is a word that describes a noun. Adjectives answer three questions:

   1. What kind is it?   **2.** How many are there?   **3.** Which one is it?

Directions: Fill in the blanks and find the answer that best completes the analogies.

1. In the word pair | **fire : hot** |, the word ___h_____ is an

  __a_____ because it tells what kind of fire it is.

2. In the word pair | **cold : ice** |, the word _____ is an

  _____ because it tells what kind of ice it is.

---

3. **tiny : ant :: big :**
- Ⓐ speck
- Ⓑ elephant
- Ⓒ large
- Ⓓ fly

4. **24 : 1 :: hours :**
- Ⓐ week
- Ⓑ year
- Ⓒ day
- Ⓓ month

5. **sandy : beach**
- Ⓐ dry : desert
- Ⓑ desert : dry
- Ⓒ ocean : swim
- Ⓓ swim : ocean

6. **cheetah : swift**
- Ⓐ whale : calf
- Ⓑ calf : whale
- Ⓒ tortoise : slow
- Ⓓ slow : tortoise

7. **months : year**
- Ⓐ 1 : 7
- Ⓑ 7 : 1
- Ⓒ 1 : 12
- Ⓓ 12 : 1

8. **sweet : candy**
- Ⓐ lemon : sour
- Ⓑ sour : lemon
- Ⓒ Earth : moon
- Ⓓ moon : Earth

---

9. Think of two adjectives that might be used to describe each noun.

  • mountain _____   _____

  • pebble _____   _____

10. Make an analogy using words and answers from question 9.

  _____ : _____ :: _____ : _____

Finding the Connection

Directions: All of the analogies below have the same connection between the word pairs. Choose the answer that best completes each analogy and answer the questions.

1. **bird : feathers**
   - Ⓐ wrapper : candy
   - Ⓑ cat : fur
   - Ⓒ crow : fly
   - Ⓓ tree : branch

2. **tree : bark**
   - Ⓐ plant : shrub
   - Ⓑ yellow : banana
   - Ⓒ frame : picture
   - Ⓓ orange : peel

3. **girl : skin**
   - Ⓐ boy : grin
   - Ⓑ high : low
   - Ⓒ fish : scales
   - Ⓓ bookcase : shelf

4. **nut : shell**
   - Ⓐ banana : peel
   - Ⓑ yellow : paint
   - Ⓒ wall : wallpaper
   - Ⓓ number : letter

5. **sandwich : bread**
   - Ⓐ crown : gold
   - Ⓑ pie : crust
   - Ⓒ hammer : nail
   - Ⓓ shell : turtle

6. **boy : cap**
   - Ⓐ bonnet : girl
   - Ⓑ crab : orange
   - Ⓒ mountain : high
   - Ⓓ king : crown

7. **gift : wrapping paper**
   - Ⓐ tablecloth : table
   - Ⓑ floor : walk
   - Ⓒ sink : dishes
   - Ⓓ pillow : pillowcase

8. **apple : skin**
   - Ⓐ Earth : planet
   - Ⓑ ocean : Earth
   - Ⓒ Earth : crust
   - Ⓓ atmosphere : Earth

9. How are all the question and correct-answer words connected or related?

   _____

10. Write your own analogy using four of these words: *oyster, nose, shell, ocean, otter, fur.*

    _____ : _____ :: _____ : _____

Finding the Connection 2

Directions: Choose the answer that best completes each analogy.

1. cat : paw
- Ⓐ dog : tail
- Ⓑ tail : dog
- Ⓒ person : foot
- Ⓓ foot : person

2. trunk : elephant
- Ⓐ snout : pig
- Ⓑ pig : snout
- Ⓒ fish : scales
- Ⓓ scales: fish

3. talon : hawk
- Ⓐ bird : feather
- Ⓑ feather : bird
- Ⓒ tiger : claw
- Ⓓ claw : tiger

4. fang : snake
- Ⓐ walrus : tusk
- Ⓑ tusk : walrus
- Ⓒ student : desk
- Ⓓ desk : student

5. boy : arm
- Ⓐ family : home
- Ⓑ zebra : stripe
- Ⓒ tree : branch
- Ⓓ giraffe : spot

6. girl : hair
- Ⓐ horse : mane
- Ⓑ grass : lawn
- Ⓒ ocean : wave
- Ⓓ sand : beach

7. turtle : shell
- Ⓐ crown : queen
- Ⓑ man : bike helmet
- Ⓒ scarf : girl
- Ⓓ boy : skateboard

8. woman : nose
- Ⓐ dolphin : fin
- Ⓑ tail : fish
- Ⓒ lobster : claw
- Ⓓ whale : blowhole

9. How are all the question and correct-answer words connected or related?

_____

10. Write your own analogy using four of these words: *wing, fish, lion, bat, big, fin.*

_____ **:** _____ **::** _____ **:** _____

Finding the Connection 3

Directions: Choose the answer that best completes each analogy.

1. **teacher : school**
   - (A) canary : fly
   - (B) fly : canary
   - (C) courtroom : judge
   - (D) judge : courtroom

2. **scarf : neck**
   - (A) hand : mitten
   - (B) mitten : hand
   - (C) moon : round
   - (D) round : moon

3. **hospital : doctor**
   - (A) classroom : student
   - (B) student : classroom
   - (C) book : pencil
   - (D) pencil : book

4. **shirt : button**
   - (A) sleeve : leg
   - (B) leg : sleeve
   - (C) pants : zipper
   - (D) zipper : pants

5. **librarian : library**
   - (A) swamp : bog
   - (B) book : read
   - (C) desert : snow
   - (D) clerk : store

6. **field : farmer**
   - (A) planet : sun
   - (B) space : astronaut
   - (C) spaceship : moon
   - (D) sun : planet

7. **earring : ear**
   - (A) coat : legs
   - (B) ocean : fish
   - (C) watch : wrist
   - (D) jungle : monkey

8. **plant : garden**
   - (A) tree : forest
   - (B) leaf : bark
   - (C) oak : acorn
   - (D) evergreen : pine

9. How are all the question and correct-answer words connected or related?

   _____

10. Write your own analogy using four of these words: *airplane, cloud, captain, pilot, ship, pool.*

   _____ : _____ :: _____ : _____

Trying Out the Connection

Directions: Write how the word pairs are connected.

1. **chocolate milk : drink**

__C_____ is a __d_____.

2. **forget : remember**

__F_____ is the opposite of __r_____.

3. **ocean : salty**

The __o_____ is __s_____.

Directions: For #4–6, fill in the words. The correct answer will be the sentence that makes sense. That is because the answer has to have the same connection as the words in the question.

4. **chocolate milk : drink**

Ⓐ **yellow : lemon**   A __y_____ is a __l_____.

Ⓑ **bird : wing**   A __b_____ is a __w_____.

Ⓒ **Dalmatian : dog**   A __D_____ is a _____.

5. **forget : remember**

Ⓐ **excite : bore**   __E_____ is the opposite of __b_____.

Ⓑ **fish : trout**   __F_____ is the opposite of __t_____.

Ⓒ **grouchy : cranky**   __G_____ is the opposite of _____.

6. **ocean : salty**

Ⓐ **fish : water**   The __f_____ is __w_____.

Ⓑ **grass : green**   The __g_____ is __g_____.

Ⓒ **green : bean**   The __g_____ is __b_____.

Part to Whole

Some word pairs in analogies are connected by "**part to whole**" or "**whole to part**."

- key : piano (*part to whole*)
- piano : key (*whole to part*)

Directions: Choose the answer that best completes each analogy and answer the questions.

1. **foot : toe**
   - (A) hand : finger
   - (B) finger : toe
   - (C) shoe : sock
   - (D) sock : shoe

2. **slice : cake**
   - (A) lemon : yellow
   - (B) yellow : lemon
   - (C) cup : lemonade
   - (D) water : lemonade

3. **day : hour**
   - (A) second : minute
   - (B) minute : second
   - (C) calendar : wall
   - (D) wall : calendar

4. **petal : flower**
   - (A) daisy : rose
   - (B) rose : daisy
   - (C) starfish : arm
   - (D) arm : starfish

5. **page : book**
   - (A) step : staircase
   - (B) staircase : step
   - (C) clown : nose
   - (D) nose : clown

6. **room : house**
   - (A) floor : roof
   - (B) roof : floor
   - (C) store : mall
   - (D) mall : store

7. **leg : knee**
   - (A) head : chest
   - (B) chest : head
   - (C) elbow : arm
   - (D) arm : elbow

8. **noodle : spaghetti**
   - (A) wall : brick
   - (B) brick : wall
   - (C) rock : stone
   - (D) stone : rock

9. By number, list the questions that were as follows:

   - "part to whole" _____2,_____

   - "whole to part" _____

10. Write an analogy using four of these words: *car, city, bicycle, classroom, building, school.*

    _____ : _____ :: _____ : _____

    Is your analogy "part to whole" or "whole to part"? _____

What People Use

Some word pairs in analogies are connected by what people use or need in their jobs.

- carpenter : hammer (*person* to *what he/she uses*)
- hammer : carpenter (*what he/she uses* to *person*)

Directions: Choose the answer that best completes each analogy and answer the questions.

1. **carpenter : hammer**
   - (A) teacher : saw
   - (B) logger : axe
   - (C) stove : cook
   - (D) hoe : gardener

2. **tractor : farmer**
   - (A) gardener : hoe
   - (B) cleaner : mop
   - (C) writer : pen
   - (D) hose : firefighter

3. **oven : baker**
   - (A) artist : paint
   - (B) carpenter : saw
   - (C) truck : driver
   - (D) teacher : chalk

4. **archer : arrow**
   - (A) student : book
   - (B) needle : tailor
   - (C) costume : actor
   - (D) bowl : cook

5. **astronaut : spacesuit**
   - (A) doctor : tractor
   - (B) painter : brush
   - (C) hoe : gardener
   - (D) shot : nurse

6. **loom : weaver**
   - (A) tailor : scissors
   - (B) scientist : microscope
   - (C) farmer : barn
   - (D) ruler : carpenter

7. **fisherman : net**
   - (A) waiter : tray
   - (B) writer : hoe
   - (C) ladder : firefighter
   - (D) siren : policewoman

8. **pick : miner**
   - (A) arrow : artist
   - (B) axe : tailor
   - (C) mitt : catcher
   - (D) vet : shot

9. Write down one of the things you might want to be or do when you grow up.

   _____

10. List five things you might use or need to do your job.

    _____

    _____

Things that Go Together

Directions: Write down what you think of when you read these words:

1. salt and _____

2. bat and _____

3. bread and _____

4. fork and _____

5. bow and _____

Check to see if the person sitting next to you or other students in your class thought of the same things.

Directions: Choose the answer that best completes the analogies. The connection between the word pairs is "things that go together."

1. **Fork** is to **knife** as **pen** is to _____.

    Ⓐ book   Ⓒ paper

    Ⓑ spoon   Ⓓ pot

2. **Salt** is to **pepper** as **stamp** is to _____.

    Ⓐ envelope   Ⓒ desk

    Ⓑ mop   Ⓓ sandwich

3. **Bat** is to **ball** as **thunder** is to _____.

    Ⓐ game   Ⓒ umbrella

    Ⓑ snow   Ⓓ lightning

4. **Bread** is to **butter** as **bride** is to _____.

    Ⓐ boom   Ⓒ broom

    Ⓑ room   Ⓓ groom

5. **Bow** is to **arrow** as **peanut butter** is to _____.

    Ⓐ pizza   Ⓒ ketchup

    Ⓑ jelly   Ⓓ ice cream

6. Make a tally mark for each student in your class. Mark how many people eat plain hotdogs. Mark how many people eat hotdogs together with something else (ketchup or mustard, for example).

Hotdogs Plain	Hotdogs with Something Else

Size and Strength

Some analogies are based on size or strength.

Directions: Choose the answer that best completes each analogy. Pay attention to order!

> **ditch : canyon** is not the same as **canyon : ditch**

1. **ditch : canyon**

  Ⓐ big : small

  Ⓑ small : big

2. **canyon : ditch**

  Ⓐ big : small

  Ⓑ small : big

3. **river : stream :: pond :**

  Ⓐ water

  Ⓑ rain

  Ⓒ glass

  Ⓓ puddle

4. **walk : run :: look :**

  Ⓐ nap

  Ⓑ stare

  Ⓒ skip

  Ⓓ hope

5. **warm : hot**

  Ⓐ sun : star

  Ⓑ star : sun

  Ⓒ cool : freezing

  Ⓓ freezing : cool

6. **road : path**

  Ⓐ car : highway

  Ⓑ highway : car

  Ⓒ hill : mountain

  Ⓓ mountain : hill

7. **sailboat : speedboat**

  Ⓐ jet : plane

  Ⓑ plane : jet

  Ⓒ tree : raft

  Ⓓ raft : tree

8. **smell : stink**

  Ⓐ old : rotten

  Ⓑ rotten : old

  Ⓒ shoes : socks

  Ⓓ socks : shoes

Directions: For #9 and #10, write down which one you think is *stronger*.

Hints: A *gale* is a very strong wind. A *hurricane* has gale-force winds.

9. gale or breeze _____

10. cloudburst or hurricane _____

Classifying Analogies

Some analogies are based on how things can be classified, or grouped.

Directions: Fill in the blanks and choose the answer that best completes each analogy.

1. How are red and blue alike?

   They are both ____c_____ .

2. How are poodles and beagles alike?

   They are both kinds of ____d_____ .

3. **Warning!** Pay attention to order: | **red : color** | is not the same as | **color : red** | !
   Red is always a color. A color is not always red.

   | **poodle : dog** | is not the same as | **dog : poodle** |

   A _____ is always a ____d_____ .

   A __d_____ is not always a __p_____ .

---

4. **Tree** is to **oak** as

   (A) **bee** is to **insect**.

   (B) **insect** is to **bee**.

5. **Elephant** is to **mammal** as

   (A) **snake** is to **reptile**.

   (B) **reptile** is to **snake**.

6. **Apple** is to **fruit** as

   (A) **pants** is to **clothes**.

   (B) **clothes** is to **pants**.

7. **Elm** is to **tree** as

   (A) **bird** is to **parakeet**.

   (B) **parakeet** is to **bird**.

8. **Dog** is to **collie** as

   (A) **trout** is to **fish**.

   (B) **fish** is to **trout**.

9. **Vegetable** is to **carrot** as

   (A) **flower** is to **daisy**.

   (B) **daisy** is to **flower**.

10. **Boa constrictor** is to **snake** as

    (A) **snake** is to **cobra**.

    (B) **cobra** is to **snake**.

11. **Spider** is to **tarantula** as

    (A) **hammer** is to **tool**.

    (B) **tool** is to **hammer**.

Classifying Analogies 2

Directions: Fill in the blanks and choose the answer that best completes each analogy.

1. How are football and baseball alike? They are both ___S_____ .

2. Why are these word pairs different? | football : sport | | sport : football |

   - ___F_____ is always a sport.

   - A ___S_____ is not always _____ .

---

3. **football : sport**
   - Ⓐ color : blue
   - Ⓑ tree : maple
   - Ⓒ banana : fruit
   - Ⓓ pie : apple

4. **mammal : cat**
   - Ⓐ insect : ladybug
   - Ⓑ minnow : fish
   - Ⓒ fly : insect
   - Ⓓ bluebird : bird

5. **pea : vegetable**
   - Ⓐ mammal : lion
   - Ⓑ flower : sunflower
   - Ⓒ fruit : apple
   - Ⓓ lizard : reptile

6. **letter : H**
   - Ⓐ 5 : number
   - Ⓑ building : house
   - Ⓒ dog : mammal
   - Ⓓ grass : plant

7. **rose : flower**
   - Ⓐ reptile : snake
   - Ⓑ fruit : strawberry
   - Ⓒ Earth : planet
   - Ⓓ tool : hammer

8. **saw : tool**
   - Ⓐ color : green
   - Ⓑ cookie : dessert
   - Ⓒ animal : elephant
   - Ⓓ bird : eagle

---

9. Write your own answer choices. Make sure only one answer choice is correct.

   | beetle : insect |

   Ⓐ _____ : animal   Ⓑ animal : _____

10. Which answer of yours was correct? Tell why.

    _____

    _____

Practice Making Classes

Directions: Think of the names of as many things as you can that fit in the given classes.

Class	Class Members or Items
1. furniture	couch,
2. instruments	
3. mammals	
4. trees	
5. birds	

Directions: Write two analogy questions using class names and some of the things you listed as members of each class. One question should list the class first, then an item. One question should list an item first, and then the class.

6. _____ : _____

   Ⓐ _____ : _____

   Ⓑ _____ : _____

   Ⓒ _____ : _____

   Ⓓ _____ : _____

Correct answer: _____

Is your answer "class to member" or "member to class"?

_____

7. _____ : _____

   Ⓐ _____ : _____

   Ⓑ _____ : _____

   Ⓒ _____ : _____

   Ⓓ _____ : _____

Correct answer: _____

Is your answer "class to member" or "member to class"?

_____

Math

Directions: Find the answer that best completes each analogy.

1. **3 + 6 : 9 :: 4 + 8 : _____**

Ⓐ 10

Ⓑ 5 + 10

Ⓒ 12

Ⓓ 13

2. **8 : 12 − 4 :: 11 : _____**

Ⓐ 14 − 3

Ⓑ 13 − 3

Ⓒ 5 + 6

Ⓓ 4 + 7

3. **卌 卌 卌 I : 16 :: 卌 卌 卌 卌 I : _____**

Ⓐ 18

Ⓑ 19

Ⓒ 20

Ⓓ 21

4. **100 : 99 + 1 :: 1,000 : _____**

Ⓐ 99 + 1

Ⓑ 999 + 1

Ⓒ 9,999 + 1

Ⓓ 99,999 + 1

5. **7 + 6 : 6 + 7 :: 9 + 4 : _____**

Ⓐ 10 + 3

Ⓑ 4 + 6

Ⓒ 9 + 13

Ⓓ 4 + 9

6. **卌 III + III : 11 :: 卌 卌 II + III : _____**

Ⓐ 14

Ⓑ 15

Ⓒ 16

Ⓓ 17

7. **25 : 50 :: 75 : _____**

Ⓐ 80

Ⓑ 90

Ⓒ 100

Ⓓ 110

8. **4 : 6 :: 10 : _____**

Ⓐ 12

Ⓑ 14

Ⓒ 16

Ⓓ 18

9. **3 : 7 :: 5 : _____**

Ⓐ 1

Ⓑ 3

Ⓒ 7

Ⓓ 9

10. **odd : 3 :: even : _____**

Ⓐ 5

Ⓑ 8

Ⓒ 9

Ⓓ 11

Math 2

Directions: Find the answer that best completes each analogy. Use the information about word beginnings to help you figure out the answers!

uni = 1	**quad** = 4	**sept** or **hept** = 7 **deca** = 10
bi = 2	**penta** = 5	**oct** = 8
tri = 3	**hex** = 6	**non** = 9

1. [bicycle image] : [unicycle image] :: **bicycle** : _____
   - (A) unicycle
   - (B) tricycle
   - (C) pentacycle
   - (D) decacycle

2. [pentagon] : **pentagon** :: [hexagon] : _____
   - (A) octogon
   - (B) nonagon
   - (C) hexagon
   - (D) triangle

3. **nonagon : decagon :: 9 :** _____
   - (A) 4
   - (B) 6
   - (C) 8
   - (D) 10

4. [square] : **quadrilateral** :: [triangle] : _____
   - (A) hexagon
   - (B) triangle
   - (C) heptagon
   - (D) pentagon

5. [octagon] : [octopus image] :: **sides :** _____
   - (A) eyes
   - (B) noses
   - (C) arms
   - (D) ears

6. [curve sign] : [STOP sign] :: **quadrilateral :** _____
   - (A) octagon
   - (B) pentagon
   - (C) nonagon
   - (D) heptagon

7. [twins image] : **twins** :: [triplets image] : _____
   - (A) octuplets
   - (B) pentuplets
   - (C) quadruplets
   - (D) triplets

8. [octagon] : **octagon** :: [nonagon] : _____
   - (A) pentagon
   - (B) heptagon
   - (C) decagon
   - (D) nonagon

Think and Write:

- How many years is a decade? _____

- If something happens bi-weekly, how often does it happen? _____

Social Studies

Directions: Find the word that best completes the analogy.

Hint: You may want to look at a more detailed world map in an atlas or on the Internet.

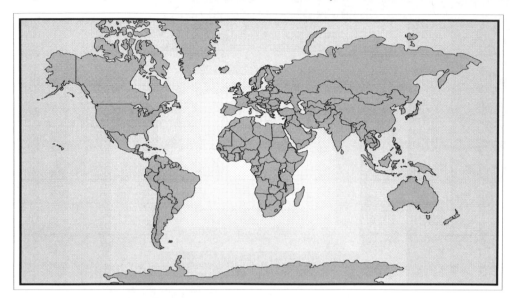

1. Kenya : Africa :: United States : _____

2. Canada : North America :: Brazil : _____

3. France : Europe :: China : _____

4. Antarctica : Antarctica :: Australia : _____

5. Mexico : North America :: Japan : _____

6. Sweden : Europe :: India : _____

7. Argentina : South America :: England : _____

8. Ecuador : South America :: Nigeria : _____

9. Zimbabwe : Africa :: Spain : _____

10. Chile : Southern Hemisphere :: United States : _____

11. Iraq : Northern Hemisphere :: New Zealand : _____

12. Peru : Southern Hemisphere :: Egypt : _____

Social Studies 2

Directions: Find the state that best completes the analogy.

Hints: You may want to use a map of the continental USA.

Answers will be *north*, *south*, *east*, or *west*.

Answers will depend on the direction each state is located in relation to the other state.

Example: | California : Nevada :: west : east | because California is west of Nevada.

1. Oregon : Washington :: south : _____

2. Colorado : New Mexico :: north : _____

3. Utah : Nevada :: east : _____

4. Oregon : Idaho :: west : _____

5. Nevada : Colorado :: west : _____

6. Montana : Wyoming :: north : _____

7. Arizona : New Mexico :: west : _____

8. Utah : Idaho : south :: _____

9. California : Oregon :: south : _____

10. Montana : Idaho :: east : _____

Challenge: Locate the states mentioned on the map and shade them with your pencil.

Science

Directions: Find the words that relate to each other in the same way the question words do.

Hints: A **carnivore** eats mostly meat.

A **herbivore** eats mostly plants.

An **omnivore** eats meat and plants.

---

1. **zebra : herbivore**

   Ⓐ lion : herbivore

   Ⓑ dog : herbivore

   Ⓒ wolf : herbivore

   Ⓓ deer : herbivore

2. **polar bear : carnivore**

   Ⓐ mouse : carnivore

   Ⓑ hawk : carnivore

   Ⓒ horse : carnivore

   Ⓓ elephant : carnivore

---

3. **cow : carnivore**

   Ⓐ tiger : carnivore

   Ⓑ shark : carnivore

   Ⓒ buffalo : carnivore

   Ⓓ owl : carnivore

4. **rabbit : omnivore**

   Ⓐ snake : herbivore

   Ⓑ cat : carnivore

   Ⓒ horse : herbivore

   Ⓓ jaguar : carnivore

---

5. **hawk : eagle**

   Ⓐ herbivore : herbivore

   Ⓑ omnivore : omnivore

   Ⓒ carnivore : carnivore

   Ⓓ carnivore : herbivore

6. **herbivore : carnivore**

   Ⓐ shark : buffalo

   Ⓑ bear : eagle

   Ⓒ mouse : rabbit

   Ⓓ giraffe : lion

Think and Write: Are you a carnivore, herbivore, or omnivore? Write down some things you eat that prove why.

I am a(n) _____ because _____

_____

_____

_____

Science 2

Directions: Use the chart about the planets in our solar system to complete the analogies.

Planet	Number from Sun	Length of One Year*
Mercury	1	88 days
Venus	2	225 days
Earth	3	365 days
Mars	4	687 days
Jupiter	5	12 years
Saturn	6	29.5 years
Uranus	7	84 years
Neptune	8	165 years
Pluto (dwarf planet)	9	248 years

A year is the time it takes for Earth to revolve around the sun once.

1. **Mercury : 88 days :: Mars : _____**

   Ⓐ 365 days   Ⓒ 84 Earth years

   Ⓑ 687 days   Ⓓ Pluto

2. **longest : shortest :: Pluto : _____**

   Ⓐ Mercury   Ⓒ Jupiter

   Ⓑ Nepture   Ⓓ Venus

3. **Nepture : Uranus :: 165 Earth years : _____**

   Ⓐ 365 days   Ⓒ 225 days

   Ⓑ 248 Earth years   Ⓓ 84 Earth years

4. **5 : 12 Earth years :: 3 : _____**

   Ⓐ 8   Ⓒ 365 days

   Ⓑ 165 days   Ⓓ 225 days

5. **shorter : longer :: Jupiter : _____**

   Ⓐ Earth   Ⓒ Neptune

   Ⓑ Venus   Ⓓ Mercury

6. **Saturn : _____ :: Venus : 2**

   Ⓐ 29.5 years   Ⓒ Jupiter

   Ⓑ 6   Ⓓ 12 years

7. If you lived on Saturn, would you be one year old yet? _____

8. If you were 1 year old on Uranus, how old would you be on Earth? _____

©*Teacher Created Resources*   35   #3166 *Analogies for Critical Thinking*

Health

Directions: Use the food pyramid to help you complete the analogies.

1. **bread : pasta :: cheese :** _____
   - (A) apple
   - (B) chips
   - (C) cookies
   - (D) milk

2. **carrots : vegetables :: grapes :** _____
   - (A) fruit
   - (B) apples
   - (C) watermelon
   - (D) corn

3. **most : bread group :: least :** _____
   - (A) fat group
   - (B) vegetable group
   - (C) fruit group
   - (D) meat group

4. **fish : eggs :: crackers :** _____
   - (A) strawberries
   - (B) corn
   - (C) flour
   - (D) ice cream

5. **cheese : milk :: oil :** _____
   - (A) ice cream
   - (B) butter
   - (C) banana
   - (D) meat

6. List a favorite thing to eat out of each group.

   1. _____   4. _____

   2. _____   5. _____

   3. _____   6. _____

Spelling

Directions: Use these spelling rules about words that end in *y* to help you complete the analogies.

- The vowels are *a, e, i, o, u,* and sometimes *y*. A consonant is any letter that is not a vowel (though *y* can be a vowel or a consonant).
- If a vowel comes before the final *y*, just add the *s* or other suffix.

  Example: boy ⟶ boys
- If a consonant comes before the final *y*, change the *y* to *i* before adding the suffix.

  Example: puppy ⟶ puppies

1. hurry : hurries :: marry : _____

2. try : tried :: cry : _____

3. toy : toys :: stay : _____

4. plenty : plentiful :: beauty : _____

5. pray : prays :: valley : _____

6. pretty : prettier :: ugly : _____

7. baby : babies :: lady : _____

8. lazy : laziness :: happy : _____

9. story : stories :: cherry : _____

10. donkey : donkeys :: monkey : _____

11. certify : certified :: mummify : _____

12. fried : frying :: tried : _____

13. muddy : muddies :: study : _____

14. play : plays :: key : _____

15. flying : flies :: denying : _____

Spelling 2

Directions: Use these spelling rules about words that end in *y* to help you answer the analogies.

- If a vowel comes before the final *y*, just add the *s* or other suffix.
- If a consonant comes before the final *y*, change the *y* to *i* before adding the suffix.
- If a verb ends in *y*, just add *ing*. (A verb is an action word like *run*, *jump*, or *see*.)

  Example: study ⟶ studying

---

1. fury : furious :: vary : _____

2. bunny : bunnies :: puppy : _____

3. fly : flying :: hurry : _____

4. delay : delays :: joy : _____

5. empty : emptying :: apply : _____

6. empty : empties :: hurry : _____

7. army : armies :: party : _____

8. happy : happiness :: busy : _____

9. try : trying :: cry : _____

10. lay : lays :: pay : _____

Challenge: Pick one of your answers. What spelling rule about words that end in *y* did you use?

_____

_____

_____

Homophones

Homophones are words that sound alike but are spelled differently and have different meanings.

Give three reasons why *ant* and *aunt* are homophones.

1. _____

2. _____

3. _____

Directions: Pick the correct homophone from the word box to complete each analogy.

ant	new	tide	weight
aunt	knew	tied	wait

4. go : leave :: stay : _____

5. eight legs : spider :: six legs : _____

6. learn : know :: learned : _____

7. big : large :: even : _____

8. brother : sister :: uncle : _____

9. air : wind :: water : _____

10. big : small :: old : _____

11. stopwatch : time :: scale : _____

Homophones 2

Homophones are words that sound alike but are spelled differently and have different meanings.

Why are *four* and *for* homophones?

1. _____

2. _____

3. _____

Directions: Pick the correct homophone from the word box to complete each analogy.

four	eight	hole	merry
for	ate	whole	marry

4. one : two :: three : _____

5. some : part :: all : _____

6. bad : good :: sad : _____

7. three : six :: four : _____

8. up : down :: against : _____

9. light : fire :: dig : _____

10. jump : leap :: wed : _____

11. sleep : slept :: eat : _____

Challenge: Can you think of at least two other homophone pairs?

_____ and _____

_____ and _____

Fun with English

English is spoken in the United States and England. Sometimes, however, the same words do not mean the same thing in both places!

Directions: Use the list to help you find the correct answer to each analogy.

American English	British English
mommy	mummy
truck	lorry
apartment	flat
car trunk	boot
car hood	bonnet
sweater	jumper
soccer	football
potato chips	crisps
fries	chips
elevator	lift
bandage	plaster

1. cut : bandage :: sore : _____

2. fries : chips :: potato chips : _____

3. road : truck :: street : _____

4. front : back :: bonnet : _____

5. house : apartment :: home : _____

6. dad : daddy :: mum : _____

7. coat : sweater :: jacket : _____

8. stairs : elevator :: steps : _____

Think and Write: Why might you want to know if you were hearing American or British English if you were told the following:

9. "Hug Mummy." _____

_____

_____

10. "Put the big box in your boot." _____

_____

_____

Review of Analogy Types

Directions: Fill in the circle next to the correct answer. On the line below, write how the word pairs are connected.

1. **pleasant : horrible**

(A) talk : listen

(B) pretty : handsome

(C) silly : funny

(D) strong : powerful

_____

(*synonym* or *antonym*)

2. **blanket : bed**

(A) napkin : towel

(B) tablecloth : table

(C) wagon : cart

(D) rug : mat

_____

(*where goes* or *big to small*)

3. **kangaroo : joey**

(A) fly : hawk

(B) rabbit : swim

(C) foal : horse

(D) seal : pup

_____

(*family name* or *animal movement*)

4. **pillow : soft**

(A) glass : clear

(B) lazy : laziness

(C) hurry : hurries

(D) white : cloud

_____

(*adjective* or *spelling*)

5. **rowed : rode**

(A) drove : sock

(B) tow : toe

(C) ate : wagon

(D) clean : brush

_____

(*adjective* or *homophone*)

6. **drummer : drum**

(A) doctor : sick

(B) teacher : student

(C) fisherman : hook

(D) car : driver

_____

(*part to whole* or *who uses*)

7. **scale : weighing**

(A) measuring : ruler

(B) ruler : flat

(C) chair : sitting

(D) table : chair

_____

(*purpose* or *adjective*)

8. **knee : leg**

(A) two : to

(B) snake : slither

(C) child : children

(D) forehead : head

_____

(*plurals* or *part to whole*)

Review of Analogy Types 2

Directions: Fill in the correct answer. On the line below, write how the word pairs are connected.

1. **blew : blow**
- Ⓐ jump : jumped
- Ⓑ drank : drink
- Ⓒ go : went
- Ⓓ forget : forgot

_____

(*plurals* or *past to present*)

2. **bracelet : wrist**
- Ⓐ finger : ring
- Ⓑ ear : earring
- Ⓒ necklace : neck
- Ⓓ jeweler : gem

_____

(*where goes* or *who uses*)

3. **allow : let**
- Ⓐ shape : mold
- Ⓑ make : ruin
- Ⓒ write : chalk
- Ⓓ carry : drop

_____

(*synonym* or *adjective*)

4. **dangerous : safe**
- Ⓐ shirt : shirts
- Ⓑ spend : save
- Ⓒ baby : infant
- Ⓓ cheat : trick

_____

(*spelling* or *antonym*)

5. **scent : sent**
- Ⓐ smell : stink
- Ⓑ fresh : old
- Ⓒ flour : flower
- Ⓓ two : pair

_____

(*homophone* or *antonym*)

6. **student : pencil**
- Ⓐ man : grandfather
- Ⓑ frying pan : cook
- Ⓒ builder : hammer
- Ⓓ ladder : steps

_____

(*who uses* or *synonym*)

7. **knife : sharp**
- Ⓐ red : strawberry
- Ⓑ purple : plum
- Ⓒ green : grape
- Ⓓ corn : yellow

_____

(*adjective* or *who uses*)

8. **eagle : bird**
- Ⓐ bean : vegetable
- Ⓑ squirrel : nut
- Ⓒ salt : pepper
- Ⓓ photo : picture

_____

(*animal movement* or *member class*)

Use What You Know

Directions: Sometimes you may not know a word. Don't give up! Go through the answer choices. Write down how the words you know are connected. Cross out the ones that do not have the same connection as the words in the question. The correct answer will be the one that is not crossed out.

How Words Are Connected

1. **light : dark**

   Ⓐ cow : milk

   Ⓑ turtle : shell

   Ⓒ terminate : begin

   Ⓓ computer : screen

   _____antonyms_____

   _____a cow gives milk_____

   _____?????_____

   _____

2. Which answer choices are *not* synonyms? _____ The answer must be _____.

3. **If something is *terminated*, it is most likely**

   Ⓐ started or turned on.   Ⓒ found or located.

   Ⓑ stopped or ended.   Ⓓ believed or thought.

How Words Are Connected

4. **small : tiny**

   Ⓐ colossal : huge

   Ⓑ tree : bark

   Ⓒ tadpole : frog

   Ⓓ giant : little

   _____?????_____

   _____

   _____

   _____

5. Which answer choices are *not* synonyms? _____ The answer must be _____.

6. **Most likely, something that is *colossal* is**

   Ⓐ round or curved.   Ⓒ rough or smooth.

   Ⓑ rare or uncommon.   Ⓓ enormous or huge.

---

7. Look up the words *terminate* and *colossal* in the dictionary. Write down what they mean.

   • terminate: _____

   • colossal: _____

Use What You Know 2

Directions: Go through the answer choices. On the line to the right, write down how the words you know are connected. Cross out the ones that do not have the same connection as the words in the question. The correct answer will be the one that is not crossed out.

1. **buck : deer**
   - Ⓐ chick : hen
   - Ⓑ fawn : deer
   - Ⓒ calf : cow
   - Ⓓ cob : swan

2. What answers do you know cannot be correct? _____, _____, _____,

3. **Most likely, a *cob* is a**
   - Ⓐ baby swan.   Ⓑ male swan.   Ⓒ female swan.   Ⓓ group of swans.

4. **herd : cattle**
   - Ⓐ quiver : cobras
   - Ⓑ dogs : pack
   - Ⓒ sheep : flock
   - Ⓓ puppies : litter

5. What answers do you know cannot be correct? _____, _____, _____,

6. **Most likely, a *quiver* is a**
   - Ⓐ male cobra.   Ⓑ baby cobra.   Ⓒ group of cobras.   Ⓓ group of swans.

7. **hen : chicken**
   - Ⓐ flyer : kangaroo
   - Ⓑ duckling : duck
   - Ⓒ cub : bear
   - Ⓓ foal : horse

8. **buffalo : herd**
   - Ⓐ horse : stallion
   - Ⓑ gosling : goose
   - Ⓒ emu : mob
   - Ⓓ flock : duck

9. **Most likely, a *flyer* is a**
   - Ⓐ male kangaroo
   - Ⓑ female kangaroo
   - Ⓒ baby kangaroo
   - Ⓓ group of kangaroos

10. **Most likely, a *mob* is a**
   - Ⓐ male emu
   - Ⓑ baby emu
   - Ⓒ female emu
   - Ⓓ group of emus

Use What You Know 3

Directions: Read all the answer choices. Think about how the words are connected and write this information on the line. **If the words in the answer choices are connected in the same way, they cannot be the answer!** This is because there is only one correct answer. Fill in the bubble next to the correct answer.

---

1. ***unknown word : unknown word***   **How Words Are Connected**

  Ⓐ colossal : big   _____

  Ⓑ cold : freezing   _____

  Ⓒ soft : hard   _____

  Ⓓ terminating : ending   _____

Answer choices _____, _____, and _____ must be wrong because they are all
_____. The correct answer is _____.

---

2. ***unknown word : unknown word***   **How Words Are Connected**

  Ⓐ two : to   _____

  Ⓑ fish : water   _____

  Ⓒ be : bee   _____

  Ⓓ sail : sale   _____

Answer choices _____, _____, and _____ must be wrong because they are all
_____. The correct answer is _____.

---

3. ***unknown word : unknown word***   **How Words Are Connected**

  Ⓐ children : child   _____

  Ⓑ potatoes : potato   _____

  Ⓒ geese : goose   _____

  Ⓓ mouse : mice   _____

Answer choices _____, _____, and _____ must be wrong because they are all
_____. The correct answer is _____.

---

4. Write down four pairs of answer choices. Make three of them the same link. See if a
   classmate can tell you what the right answer is!

  Ⓐ _____ : _____   Ⓒ _____ : _____

  Ⓑ _____ : _____   Ⓓ _____ : _____

Use What You Know 4

Sometimes you may not know a word in the question. Don't give up! You may still be able to find the answer by using what you know.

Directions: Read all the answer choices. Think about how the words are connected. **If the words in the answer choices are connected in the same way, they cannot be the answer!** This is because there is only one correct answer. Fill in the bubble next to the correct answer.

How Words Are Connected

1. *unknown word : unknown word*
   - Ⓐ hurry : rush   synonyms
   - Ⓑ run : crawl
   - Ⓒ nap : sleep
   - Ⓓ buy : shop

   Answer choices _____, _____, and _____ must be wrong because they

   are all _____. The correct answer is _____.

2. *unknown word : unknown word*
   - Ⓐ sing : song
   - Ⓑ beat : drum
   - Ⓒ laugh : giggle
   - Ⓓ strum : guitar

3. *unknown word : unknown word*
   - Ⓐ buy : bought
   - Ⓑ weigh : way
   - Ⓒ here : hear
   - Ⓓ flea : flee

4. **ocelot : cat**
   - Ⓐ bright : star
   - Ⓑ red : apple
   - Ⓒ wet : swamp
   - Ⓓ hound : dog

5. **peaceful : pacific**
   - Ⓐ high : low
   - Ⓑ fright : scare
   - Ⓒ exit : enter
   - Ⓓ weep : laugh

6. Most likely, an ocelot is a kind of _____.

7. Most likely, if something is pacific, it is _____.

8. Do you think the explorer who named the Pacific Ocean saw it first on a calm or

   stormy day? _____

Analogies in Writing

An analogy is a likeness in some ways between things that are otherwise unlike. Writers often use analogies. They use them to help the reader make pictures in their heads.

Example: A fawn is a baby deer. A girl is a young person.

Write down two ways a girl might be like a fawn.

1. _____

2. _____

Directions: Complete the following sentence by choosing one answer from each set:

If a writer compares a girl to a fawn, the writer may want the reader to make a picture in his or her head of a . . .

3.
Ⓐ girl with long legs.

Ⓑ girl with short legs.

4.
Ⓐ girl who likes the noise of a city.

Ⓑ girl who likes the quiet of the forest.

5.
Ⓐ shy girl.

Ⓑ girl who is not shy.

6.
Ⓐ girl who can't leap or run.

Ⓑ girl who can leap and run fast.

Think and Write: Pick someone to use in an analogy. Tell how they are like the sun.

_____ is like the sun because _____

_____

_____

_____

_____

Analogies in Writing 2

Remember that an analogy is a likeness in some ways between things that are otherwise unlike.

Directions: Complete the sentence and write more sentences to finish the analogies.

1. Cars are like ants because _____

_____

_____

_____

_____

2. Going to the library is like mining for gold because _____

_____

_____

_____

_____

3. A rainforest is like an orchestra because _____

_____

_____

_____

_____

4. The ocean is like another planet because _____

_____

_____

_____

_____

Now share one of your analogies with the class.

Far Out Analogies

Directions: Think outside the box! Make up analogies that are so far out that they are silly. Have fun and be creative!

Example: | bike : ice cream as car : cheese |

Link: You don't want to ride a bike made out of ice cream, just like you don't want to ride in a car made out of cheese!

Example: | purple : ear as green : nose |

Link: Purple ears are strange, just as green noses are strange!

1. **ketchup : wall** as **jelly :** _____

   Link: _____

2. **open window : submarine** as _____ : _____

   Link: _____

3. **plate : teeth** as _____ : _____

   Link: _____

4. **dinosaur : kitchen** as _____ : _____

   Link: _____

5. **computer : eat** as _____ : _____

   Link: _____

6. _____ : _____ as _____ : _____

   Link: _____

Analogies in Reading

Directions: Read the passage. Answer the questions below.

"My house was a zoo this morning," said Ben. "My dad was mad! He couldn't find his glasses, so he was roaring like a lion. Then my grandma started to laugh. She laughed like a hyena. Then my brother started to hoot. He hooted like an owl. Then my dog started to howl. That made the cat start meowing. It was so noisy, my dad could barely hear what I needed to say."

"What did you need to say?" asked Maria.

"I needed to tell my dad that his glasses were on top of his head!"

1. **Most likely, Ben said his house was a zoo because**

   Ⓐ his father was a zookeeper.

   Ⓑ he lived in a house in the zoo.

   Ⓒ dogs and cats are in some zoos.

   Ⓓ animals in zoos make a lot of noise.

2. **Why did Ben say his brother was like an owl?**

   Ⓐ They both howl.

   Ⓑ They both roar.

   Ⓒ They both hoot.

   Ⓓ They both meow.

3. **Think about your house or your classroom. Give two reasons why it might be like something else. It could be like a zoo, circus, pond, book, spaceship, or whatever you want.**

   My _____ is like a _____

   _____

   _____

   _____

Analogies in Reading 2

Directions: Read the passage. Answer the questions below.

Ms. Brown said, "I have something. I have it right now. Do you know what it is? Try to guess." No one knew, so Ms. Brown continued, "I will give you a hint. I am sitting down, but when I stand up, I won't have it anymore. What is it? What do I have?"

The children thought and thought. They were in the dark. They could not guess what Ms. Brown had.

Then, a light bulb went on! The children knew. "We know what you have when you are sitting down," they said. "We know what you lose when you stand up!"

"What is it?" asked Ms. Brown.

"It's your lap!" shouted all the children. "You have a lap when you sit down, but you lose it when you stand up."

1. **The light going on was an analogy to the children**

   Ⓐ standing up.　　　　　Ⓒ losing their laps.

   Ⓑ getting bright ideas.　　Ⓓ getting lost in the dark.

2. **In the beginning of the story, the children felt as if they were in the dark because**

   Ⓐ the classroom was dark.

   Ⓑ Ms. Brown hadn't turned on the lights yet.

   Ⓒ they didn't know what Ms. Brown had.

   Ⓓ Ms. Brown told the children what it was she had.

3. **Write about a time when you felt as if you were in the dark or a light bulb went off.**

   _____

   _____

   _____

   _____

   _____

   _____

Analogies in Reading 3

Directions: Read the passage. Answer the questions below.

"My cat is an alarm clock," Kim said. "Every morning it wakes me up. It comes into my room at 7:00 a.m. It jumps on my belly. It walks up and down my chest. It meows and meows. It will not stop until I get up."

"That's great!" said Jerome. "I like your alarm clock!"

"There is only one problem," said Kim.

"What's that?" asked Jerome.

"My cat may know how to tell time, but it does not know what day of the week it is. It does not know when It Is the weekend. It does not know that on Saturday and Sunday I can stay in bed. I do not have to get up at 7:00 a.m."

"What your cat needs," said Jerome laughing, "is a calendar!"

1. **Kim's cat is like an alarm clock because**

   Ⓐ it jumps on her belly.

   Ⓑ it tells her when to get up.

   Ⓒ it walks up and down her chest.

   Ⓓ it knows what day of the week it is.

Directions: Complete the analogies.

2. **Saturday : weekend**

   Ⓐ cat : problem   Ⓒ school day : Monday

   Ⓑ problem : cat   Ⓓ Monday : school day

3. **clock : time**

   Ⓐ year : hour   Ⓒ calendar : day

   Ⓑ alarm : Saturday   Ⓓ month : week

4. **Answer these questions:**

   • What time do you get up on a school day? _____

   • What time do you get up on a Saturday? _____

   • How do you know when to wake up? _____

Connection Review

Directions: Look at the word pairs in the first column. Think about how they are connected. Try to match the word pairs with a phrase from the second column that tells how they are connected.

Use each phrase only once. The first one has been done for you.

Hint: If you do not know an answer right away, skip it. Come back to it at the end.

Word Pairs		How They Are Connected
J	1. **sink** to **kitchen**	**A.** antonym (opposite)
	2. **sea** to **see**	**B.** synonym (same meaning)
	3. **ox** to **oxen**	**C.** homophone (same sound)
	4. **fix** to **break**	**D.** adjective
	5. **fruit** to **orange**	**E.** classifying (whole to part)
	6. **bird** to **chirp**	**F.** past to present
	7. **cities** to **city**	**G.** one (singular) to more than one (plural)
	8. **mix** to **stir**	**H.** more than one (plural) to one (singular)
	9. **table** to **chairs**	**I.** purpose
	10. **snow** to **white**	**J.** where things go
	11. **ruler** to **measure**	**K.** things that go together
	12. **paid** to **pay**	**L.** animal sounds

Connection Review 2

Directions: Look at the word pairs in the first column. Think about how they are connected. Try to match the word pairs with a phrase from the second column that tells how they are connected.

Use each phrase only once. The first one has been done for you.

Hint: If you do not know an answer right away, skip it. Come back to it at the end.

Word Pairs	How They Are Connected
K 1. **pond** to **lake**	**A.** antonym (opposite)
_____ 2. **cloud** : **fluffy**	**B.** synonym (same meaning)
_____ 3. **otter** to **swims**	**C.** homophone (same sound)
_____ 4. **cheerful** to **jolly**	**D.** adjective
_____ 5. **knight** to **sword**	**E.** family names
_____ 6. **brave** to **cowardly**	**F.** what people use
_____ 7. **wrapper** to **gum**	**G.** part of something
_____ 8. **dear** to **deer**	**H.** animal movement
_____ 9. **mountain** to **hill**	**I.** outside or on top
_____ 10. **doe** to **fawn**	**J.** classifying (whole to part)
_____ 11. **carnivores** to **owls**	**K.** small to big
_____ 12. **branch** : **tree**	**L.** big to small

Practice Being the Teacher

Directions: It is your turn to teach. Look at the word pair. Show how to find the answer to the analogy.

> **surprises : amazes**

   Ⓐ floats : sinks   Ⓒ shoves : pushes

   Ⓑ shocks : insects   Ⓓ empties : fills

1. Write out how the words in the box are connected.

- When something ____s____ , it ____a____ .

Try out the connection with the other word pairs.

   Ⓐ When something ____f____ , it ____s____ .

   Ⓑ When something ____s____ , it ____i____ .

   Ⓒ When something ____s____ , it ____p____ .

   Ⓓ When something ____e____ , it ____f____ .

2. Answers _____ and _____ cannot be right because they have the same connection. They are both _____ .
                                        (*synonyms* or *antonyms*)

3. Answer _____ cannot be right because the words in the word pair are not _____ .
           (*synonyms* or *antonyms*)

---

4. Fill in the circle next to the answer for this word pair:

> **child : kittens**

   Ⓐ puppies : duckling   Ⓒ cow : chicks

   Ⓑ goslings : geese   Ⓓ lamb : calves

5. Answers _____ and _____ are wrong because the first word is plural (more than one).

6. Answer _____ is wrong because the first word is not the name of a baby or young one.

Practice Being the Teacher 2

Directions: It is your turn to teach. Look at the word pair. Show how to find the answer to the analogy.

turn : key

(A) unlock : open   (C) save : help

(B) ball : kick   (D) pedal : bicycle

1. Write out how the words in the box are connected.

- You __t_____ a __k_____.

Try out the connection with the other word pairs.

(A) You __u_____ an __o_____.

(B) You __b_____ a __k_____.

(C) You __s_____ a __h_____.

(D) You __p_____ a __b_____.

2. Answers _____ and _____ cannot be right because

they have the same connection. They are both _____.
(*synonyms* or *antonyms*)

3. Answer _____ cannot be right because it is in the wrong order.

---

4. Fill in the circle next to the answer for this word pair:

circle : shape

(A) tree : oak   (C) pansy : flower

(B) lions : animal   (D) food : cracker

5. Answer _____ is wrong because the first one is plural (more than one).

6. Answers _____ and _____ are wrong because they are written in the wrong order.

Practice What You Know

Directions: Find the answer that best completes each analogy. Remember the following:

- Pay attention to word order and spelling.
- Think about how the words are connected.
- Read every answer choice. Cross out the ones that can't be right.

---

1. **tumble : fall**
- Ⓐ throw : catch
- Ⓑ find : discover
- Ⓒ tick : tock
- Ⓓ scamper : stay

2. **complain : compliment**
- Ⓐ gaze : look
- Ⓑ know : learn
- Ⓒ enjoy : dislike
- Ⓓ jump : leap

3. **heal : real**
- Ⓐ heel : reel
- Ⓑ foot : toe
- Ⓒ mend : dance
- Ⓓ true : doctor

4. **women : woman**
- Ⓐ toe : toes
- Ⓑ potato : potatoes
- Ⓒ volcanos : volcano
- Ⓓ tomatoes: tomato

5. **dog : leash**
- Ⓐ cat : purr
- Ⓑ zebra : stripes
- Ⓒ horse : reins
- Ⓓ cow : saddle

6. **heard : herd**
- Ⓐ slept : group
- Ⓑ played : few
- Ⓒ rained : many
- Ⓓ listened : bunch

7. **poet : poem**
- Ⓐ baker : cookie
- Ⓑ picture : painter
- Ⓒ rug : weaver
- Ⓓ word : letter

8. **bathing suit : swim**
- Ⓐ suit : tie
- Ⓑ snowsuit : ski
- Ⓒ shirt : clothes
- Ⓓ pajamas : school

---

9. Make an analogy with your name and the number of letters in it. Use classmates' names for answer choices. Only one answer should be correct.

_____ : _____
 (*your name*)   (*number of letters*)

Ⓐ _____ : _____   Ⓒ _____ : _____

Ⓑ _____ : _____   Ⓓ _____ : _____

10. Tell which answer of yours was correct and why. _____

_____

Practice What You Know 2

Directions: Find the answer that best completes each analogy. Remember the following:

- Pay attention to word order and spelling.
- Think about how the words are connected.
- Read every answer choice. Cross out the ones that can't be right.

1. **bases : baseball**
   - Ⓐ football : tennis
   - Ⓑ tag : run
   - Ⓒ nets : basketball
   - Ⓓ soccer : goals

2. **bell : rings**
   - Ⓐ wolf : wolves
   - Ⓑ wolf : pups
   - Ⓒ wolf : wild
   - Ⓓ wolf : howls

3. **shiver : shake**
   - Ⓐ flour : cake
   - Ⓑ spot : see
   - Ⓒ sky : ground
   - Ⓓ write : paper

4. **leaves : rake**
   - Ⓐ weeds : hoe
   - Ⓑ saw : trees
   - Ⓒ slice : bread
   - Ⓓ train : track

5. **window : wall**
   - Ⓐ bed : kitchen
   - Ⓑ picture : floor
   - Ⓒ frame : glass
   - Ⓓ skylight : ceiling

6. **tasty : delicious**
   - Ⓐ spicy : hot
   - Ⓑ sour : sweet
   - Ⓒ icy : warm
   - Ⓓ mushy : hard

7. **emptied : empty**
   - Ⓐ try : tried
   - Ⓑ tried : try
   - Ⓒ try : tryed
   - Ⓓ tryed : try

8. **mice : mouse**
   - Ⓐ gooses : goose
   - Ⓑ fox : foxes
   - Ⓒ feet : foot
   - Ⓓ tooths : tooth

9. Make answer choices for the word pair below. Make sure only one answer choice is correct.

strong : weak

   Ⓐ _____ : _____   Ⓒ _____ : _____

   Ⓑ _____ : _____   Ⓓ _____ : _____

10. Tell which answer of yours was correct and why. _____

_____

Answer Sheets

These sheets may be used to provide practice in answering questions in a standardized-test format.

Student's Name: _____

_____

Activity Page: _____

1.   Ⓐ   Ⓑ   Ⓒ   Ⓓ

2.   Ⓐ   Ⓑ   Ⓒ   Ⓓ

3.   Ⓐ   Ⓑ   Ⓒ   Ⓓ

4.   Ⓐ   Ⓑ   Ⓒ   Ⓓ

5.   Ⓐ   Ⓑ   Ⓒ   Ⓓ

6.   Ⓐ   Ⓑ   Ⓒ   Ⓓ

7.   Ⓐ   Ⓑ   Ⓒ   Ⓓ

8.   Ⓐ   Ⓑ   Ⓒ   Ⓓ

9.   Ⓐ   Ⓑ   Ⓒ   Ⓓ

10.   Ⓐ   Ⓑ   Ⓒ   Ⓓ

Student's Name: _____

_____

Activity Page: _____

1.   Ⓐ   Ⓑ   Ⓒ   Ⓓ

2.   Ⓐ   Ⓑ   Ⓒ   Ⓓ

3.   Ⓐ   Ⓑ   Ⓒ   Ⓓ

4.   Ⓐ   Ⓑ   Ⓒ   Ⓓ

5.   Ⓐ   Ⓑ   Ⓒ   Ⓓ

6.   Ⓐ   Ⓑ   Ⓒ   Ⓓ

7.   Ⓐ   Ⓑ   Ⓒ   Ⓓ

8.   Ⓐ   Ⓑ   Ⓒ   Ⓓ

9.   Ⓐ   Ⓑ   Ⓒ   Ⓓ

10.   Ⓐ   Ⓑ   Ⓒ   Ⓓ

Answer Key

Introducing Analogies (page 4)
1. puppy
2. bark
3. foot
4. feathers
5. wild
7. father
8. mom
9. aunt
10. woman

Synonyms in Analogies (page 5)
1. C
2. B
3. D
4. C
5. A
6. D
7. A
8. D

Antonyms in Analogies (page 6)
1. D
2. A
3. B
4. D
5. C
6. B
7. C
8. A

Synonym and Antonym Practice (page 7)
1. D, synonym
2. D, antonym
3. A, antonym
4. C, synonym
5. B, synonym
6. B, antonym
7. C, antonym
8. A, synonym

Writing Synonym and Antonym Analogies (page 8)
Accept reasonable responses.

Plurals (page 9)
1. tomatoes
2. halves
3. wolves
4. knives
5. loaves
6. volcanoes
7. thieves
8. elves
9. hooves
10. heroes
11. 7

Plurals 2 (page 10)
1. child : children or men : man
2. B
3. D
4. A
5. C
6. C
7. A
8. D
9. B
10. houses

A Trip to the Zoo (page 11)
1. A
2. B
3. D
4. A
5. B
6. C
7. A
8. C
9. D
10. D

Animals on the Loose (page 12)
1. B
2. A
3. A
4. C
5. B
6. D
7. B
8. D
9. B
10. C

Past and Present (page 13)
1. taught
2. gazed
3. see
4. bled
5. find
6. searched
7. hurt
8. walk
9. rose
10. speed
11. present to past: 1, 2, 4, 6, 9; past to present: 3, 5, 8, 10; impossible to tell: 7; synonym: 2

Past and Present 2 (page 14)
1. A
2. B
3. B
4. C
5. A
6. C
7. D
8. A

Purpose (page 15)
1. A
2. B
3. C
4. D
5. B
6. D
7. A
8. C

Where Things Go (page 16)
1. B
2. A
3. D
4. A
5. C
6. A
7. B
8. D

Family Names (page 17)
1. A
2. B
3. A
4. B
5. D
6. B
7. C
8. A

Adjectives (page 18)
1. hot, adjective
2. cold, adjective
3. B
4. C
5. A
6. C
7. D
8. B

Finding the Connection (page 19)
1. B
2. D
3. C
4. A
5. B
6. D
7. D
8. C
9. They each deal with a covering or something outside of something else.
10. oyster : shell :: otter : fur

Answer Key (cont.)

Finding the Connection 2 (page 20)

1. C 5. C
2. A 6. A
3. D 7. B
4. B 8. D
9. They all serve the same purpose or are attached in the same way.
10. bat : wing :: fish : fin (order may be reversed)

Finding the Connection 3 (page 21)

1. D 5. D
2. B 6. B
3. A 7. C
4. C 8. A
9. They all deal with where something or somebody is or can be found.
10. airplane : pilot :: ship : captain (order may be reversed)

Trying Out the Connection (page 22)

1. Chocolate milk is a drink.
2. Forget is the opposite of remember.
3. The ocean is salty.
4. C
5. A
6. B

Part to Whole (page 23)

1. A 5. A
2. C 6. C
3. B 7. D
4. D 8. B
9. part to whole: 2, 4, 5, 6, 8; whole to part: 1, 3, 7
10. building : city :: classroom : school (answers may be reversed)

What People Use (page 24)

1. B 5. B
2. D 6. D
3. C 7. A
4. A 8. C

Things that Go Together (page 25)

1. C 4. D
2. A 5. B
3. D

Size and Strength (page 26)

1. B 6. D
2. A 7. B
3. D 8. A
4. B 9. gale
5. C 10. hurricane

Classifying Analogies (page 27)

1. colors
2. dogs
3. A poodle is always a dog. A dog is not always a poodle.
4. B 8. B
5. A 9. A
6. A 10. B
7. B 11. B

Classifying Analogies 2 (page 28)

1. sports
2. Football is always a sport. A sport is not always football.
3. C
4. A
5. D
6. B
7. C
8. B
10. Answer choice A is correct because a beetle is a kind of insect. An insect is not a kind of beetle.

Practice Making Classes (page 29)

Accept reasonable responses.

Math (page 30)

1. C 6. B
2. A 7. C
3. D 8. A
4. B 9. D
5. D 10. B

Math 2 (page 31)

1. A 5. C
2. C 6. A
3. D 7. D
4. B 8. D

Think and Write: 10; twice a week

Social Studies (page 32)

1. North America
2. South America
3. Asia
4. Australia
5. Asia
6. Asia
7. Europe
8. Africa
9. Europe
10. Northern Hemisphere
11. Southern Hemisphere
12. Northern Hemisphere

Social Studies 2 (page 33)

1. north 6. south
2. south 7. east
3. west 8. north
4. east 9. north
5. east 10. west

Science (page 34)

1. D 4. A
2. B 5. C
3. C 6. D

Answer Key (cont.)

Science 2 (page 35)

1. B
2. A
3. D
4. C
5. C
6. B
7. no
8. 84

Health (page 36)

1. D
2. A
3. A
4. C
5. B

Spelling (page 37)

1. marries
2. cried
3. stays
4. beautiful
5. valleys
6. uglier
7. ladies
8. happiness
9. cherries
10. monkeys
11. mummified
12. trying
13. studies
14. keys
15. denies

Spelling 2 (page 38)

1. various
2. puppies
3. hurrying
4. joys
5. applying
6. hurries
7. parties
8. business
9. crying
10. pays

Homophones (page 39)

1–3. sound alike, spelled differently, different meanings
4. wait
5. ant
6. knew
7. tied
8. aunt
9. tide
10. new
11. weight

Homophones 2 (page 40)

1–3. sound alike, spelled differently, different meanings
4. four
5. whole
6. merry
7. eight
8. for
9. hole
10. marry
11. ate

Fun with English (page 41)

1. plaster
2. crisps
3. lorry
4. boot
5. flat
6. mummy
7. jumper
8. lift

Review of Analogy Types (page 42)

1. A, antonym
2. B, where goes
3. D, family name
4. A, adjective
5. B, homophone
6. C, who uses
7. C, purpose
8. D, part to whole

Review of Analogy Types 2 (page 43)

1. B, past to present
2. C, where goes
3. A, synonym
4. B, antonym
5. C, homophone
6. C, who uses
7. D, adjective
8. A, member class

Use What You Know (page 44)

1. antonyms; A. a cow gives milk; B. a turtle has a shell; C. a computer has a screen.
2. A, B, D; C
3. B
4. synonyms; A. words are synonyms; B. a tree is covered in bark; C. a tadpole grows into a frog; D. words are antonyms.
5. B, C, D; A
6. D
7. terminate: to end, to finish; colossal: huge, enormous

Use What You Know 2 (page 45)

1. male deer to deer; A. baby to mother; B. baby to mother; C. baby to mother; D. male swan to swan.
2. A, B, C
3. B
4. a herd is a group of cattle; A. quiver is a group of cobras; B. dogs make up a pack; C. a lamb is a baby sheep; D. puppies make up a litter.
5. B, C, D
6. C
7. A
8. C
9. B
10. D

Answer Key *(cont.)*

Use What You Know 3 (page 46)

1. wrong (all synonyms): A, B, D; correct (antonym): C
2. wrong (all homophones): A, C, D; correct (where found): B
3. wrong (all plural to singular): A, B, C; correct (singular to plural): D

Use What You Know 4 (page 47)

1. wrong (all synonyms): A, C, D; correct (antonym): B
2. C
3. A
4. D
5. B
6. cat
7. peaceful
8. calm

Analogies in Writing (page 48)

1.–2. Accept reasonable responses.
3. A
4. B
5. A
6. B

Analogies in Writing 2 (page 49)

Accept reasonable responses.

Far Out Analogies (page 50)

Accept reasonable responses.

Analogies in Reading (page 51)

1. D
2. C
3. Accept reasonable responses.

Analogies in Reading 2 (page 52)

1. B
2. C
3. Accept reasonable responses.

Analogies in Reading 3 (page 53)

1. B
2. D
3. C

Connection Review (page 54)

1. J
2. C
3. G
4. A
5. E
6. L
7. H
8. B
9. K
10. D
11. I
12. F

Connection Review 2 (page 55)

1. K
2. D
3. H
4. B
5. F
6. A
7. I
8. C
9. L
10. E
11. J
12. G

Practice Being the Teacher (page 56)

1. When something surprises, it amazes; A: When something floats, it sinks; B: When something shocks, it insects; C: When something shoves, it pushes; D: When something empties, it fills.
2. A and D, antonyms
3. B, synonyms
4. D
5. A and B
6. C

Practice Being the Teacher 2 (page 57)

1. You turn a key; A: You unlock an open; B: You ball a kick; C: You save a help; D: You pedal a bicycle.
2. A and C, synonyms
3. B
4. C
5. B
6. A and D

Practice What You Know (page 58)

1. B
2. C
3. A
4. D
5. C
6. D
7. A
8. B

Practice What You Know 2 (page 59)

1. C
2. D
3. B
4. A
5. D
6. A
7. B
8. C

Made in the USA
Middletown, DE
12 December 2022

18234499R00038